MORE PRAISE FOR BABYMOUSE!

"Sassy, smart . . . Babymouse is here to stay."
—The Horn Book Magazine

"Young readers will happily fall in line."
—Kirkus Reviews

"The brother-sister creative team hits the mark with humor, sweetness, and characters so genuine they can pass for real kids." —Booklist

"Babymouse is spunky, ambitious, and, at times, a total dweeb."
—School Library Journal

Fall in love with **all** the **BABYMOUSE** books!

BABYMOUSE
HEARTBREAKER

BY JENNIFER L. HOLM & MATTHEW HOLM

RANDOM HOUSE NEW YORK

This is a work of fiction. Names, characters, places, and incidents either are the product of the authors' imagination or are used fictitiously. Any resemblance to actual persons, living or dead, events, or locales is entirely coincidental.

Copyright © 2006 by Jennifer Holm and Matthew Holm

Published in the United States by Random House Children's Books, a division of Random House, Inc., New York.

RANDOM HOUSE and colophon are registered trademarks of Random House, Inc.

www.randomhouse.com/kids
www.babymouse.com

Educators and librarians, for a variety of teaching tools, visit us at www.randomhouse.com/teachers

Library of Congress Cataloging-in-Publication Data
Holm, Jennifer L.
Babymouse : Heartbreaker / Jennifer L. Holm and Matthew Holm.
   p.   cm.
ISBN 978-0-375-83798-2 (trade) — ISBN 978-0-375-93798-9 (lib. bdg.)
I. Graphic novels. I. Holm, Matthew. II. Title.
PN6727.H592B27 2006
741.5'973—dc22
2006045418

PRINTED IN MALAYSIA   16 15 14 13 12 11 10 9 8

...WITH ROMANCE!

BABYMOUSE, BABYMOUSE, WHEREFORE ART THOU FAIR BABYMOUSE?

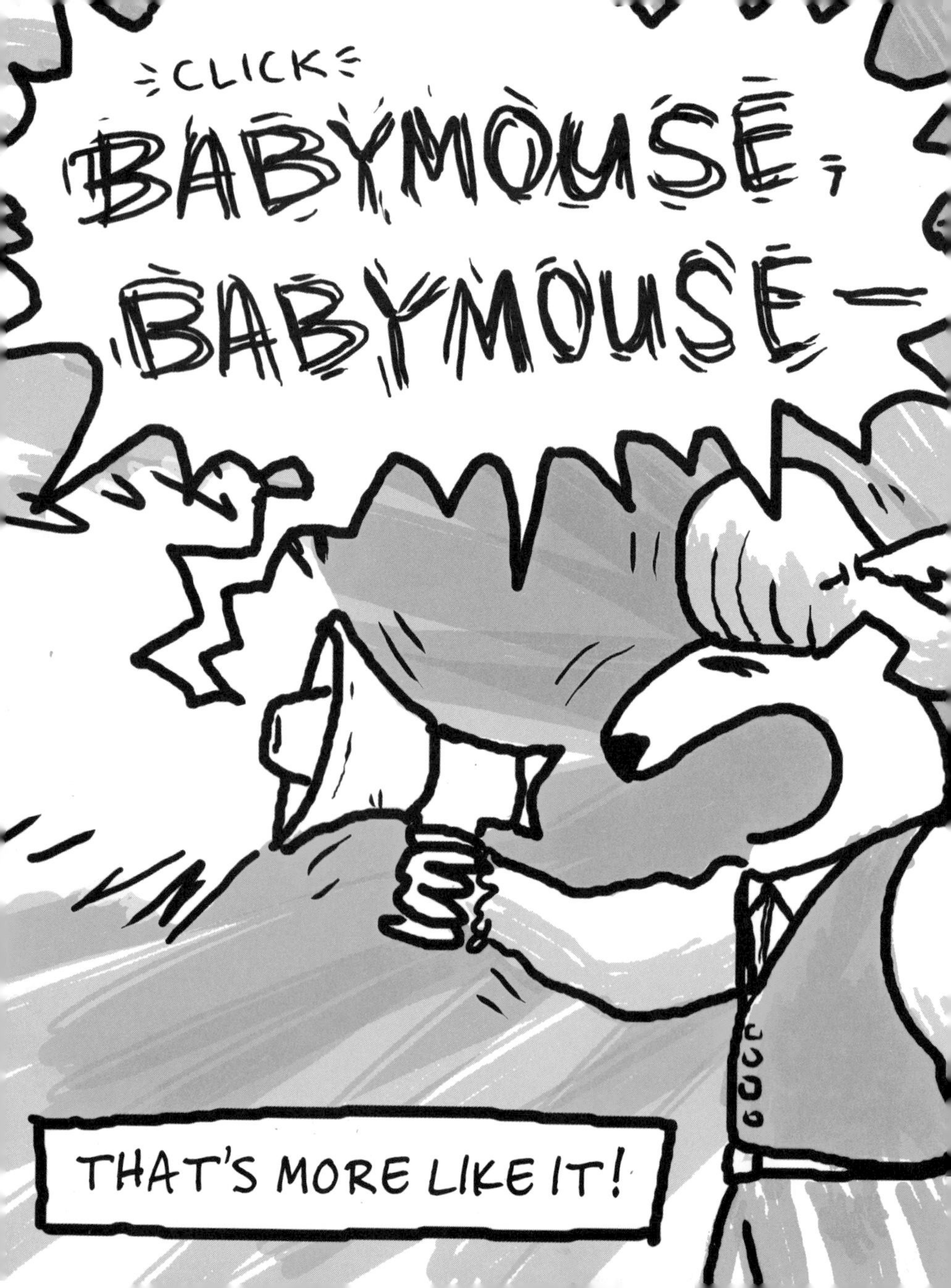
CLICK
BABYMOUSE,
BABYMOUSE—
THAT'S MORE LIKE IT!

15

WAIT A MINUTE. DIDN'T WE HAVE A BABYMOUSERELLA FANTASY IN THE FIRST BOOK?

YEAH, WELL, I NEVER EVEN MADE IT TO THE DANCE LAST TIME!

BONG! BONG!

OH NO! TIME TO GO!

BONG! BONG!

43

44

YOU'RE SAYING A FROG TRICKED YOU INTO KISSING HIM AND HE TURNED INTO A SNAKE AND THEN A SNAIL AND THEN A SPIDER WHO WAS A SPIDER-PRINCE, AND THAT'S WHY YOU'RE LATE FOR CLASS?
I DON'T KNOW WHY I EVEN BOTHER EXPLAINING.

THE NEXT DAY AFTER SCHOOL.

Rx PHARMACY

OPEN

OPEN

Thanks for shopping.

LIPSTICK

BLUSH

WHISKER COLOR

EYE SHADOW

MASCARA

Thanks for shopping

WHAT ARE YOU DOING, BABYMOUSE?

A MAKEOVER! THIS ARTICLE GUARANTEES I'LL BE "UNFORGETTABLE" TO BOYS. I'LL GET ASKED TO THE DANCE IN NO TIME!

[I don't know, Commander — he was looking at something on Earth and he just fell over!]

54

61

THE CLOCK WAS TICKING.

TICK
TICK

SECRET AGENT 003½ KNEW THE IMPORTANCE OF HER MISSION...

...AND OF LOOKING GOOD.

I LOOK GOOD!

THERE WAS NO TIME TO LOSE...

SHE ZEROED IN...

OH DEAR.

WELL, YOU COULD ALWAYS DANCE WITH YOUR TEACHER, BABYMOUSE.

TYPICAL.

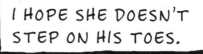